Tab

Conclusion

Dedication

This book is dedicated to my grandmother Minnie Lee Johns for without her this book would not be possible. Thank you for everything.

Preface

The idea for this book came from my grandmother. While living in Spain, I had no idea I would write a book about the country. One day my grandmother suggested that I write a book to help other people who might be in my position, so that if they decided to come to Spain, they would not be as lost or confused as I once was, and they would have the information needed to navigate this beautiful and rich country as a foreigner.

Introduction

Five years ago, I made a decision that would change my life forever. I was living in Seattle daydreaming about living in Europe (I've always wanted to live in Europe). One day I decided to pack my bags, leave the U.S. for good and never look back. I picked Spain as my new home because my late paternal grandmother was Spanish. We were very close and this motivated me to save money and take a risk which I don't regret doing.

I didn't know anything about Spain when I first arrived. I didn't speak Spanish and had no job, friends, or family. I was completely alone and had no clue what I was doing. I learned how to make friends. learn the language, find work, and navigate through a foreign country that feels like an entirely different world.

This book is your guide to moving to Spain should you want to make the transition. My maternal grandmother gave me the idea for this book as a way to help others so that they won't be in the same situation as I once was. I will do my best to share my knowledge and personal firsthand experience. Although you should understand that some of the information may change after the date this book has been published. The Spanish government is always making changes to how the country operates.

After you've read the book, I hope that I can help remove any fear or doubt you may have about moving to Spain. It can indeed be scary and stressful if you have never lived abroad. However, it can also be a wonderful life-changing experience with new possibilities and opportunities.

Chapter 1

Why Spain?

Some of you may be wondering why bother moving to Spain when there are tons of beautiful countries to choose from. Well, this is a good question to ask because it's true. There are so many beautiful countries to visit as well as to live in. It should also be noted that some countries may be suited for you based on your lifestyle, personality, and income. I have traveled to many countries, but only for vacation or work. Spain is the only country that I have ever lived in besides my home country of course.

There are several reasons why I recommend living in Spain. The people are fantastic and very social. I'm an introvert and generally find talking to be a chore. I'm one of those people that prefer a text instead of a call. However, the people in Spain are so friendly and open-minded that I don't mind being a little social here and there. It's very easy to make friends in Spain as people will go out of their way to get to know you even if you don't speak the language. Before I learned Spanish people would use google translate to start a conversation with me and I thought it was wonderful.

The Weather

In addition to the social life and friendly atmosphere, the weather is wonderful. Spain has some of the best weather in Southern Europe. Speaking about the climate, if you prefer colder temperatures then you might want to move to the north of Spain.

The north has more rainy days and snowy winters in some places, but the landscapes are green and lush.

If you prefer extreme temperatures as in really hot in the summer and cold in the winter then you may want to check out central Spain. Madrid is one city with extreme temperatures with no middle ground (unless climate change fixes that). I did enjoy living in Madrid, but they don't have a beach which was a bummer.

If you enjoy really hot weather and hate the cold you might find the south of Spain to be more to your liking, especially Seville. I have been there a few times and oh my goodness it's hot! The temperatures can reach 116 degrees Fahrenheit in the summer.

If you want nice warm mild temperatures all year around then the Canary Islands is where you want to be. I have been living in the Canary Islands for more than 4 years now and the temperatures are incredible. You're looking at temperatures between 72 to 80 throughout the year. The Canary Islands are located next to North Africa so they share subtropical weather. There are some exceptions though. There are seven Islands of the Canaries and some of them do have rain, mostly islands like La Palma, La Gomera, El Hierro, and the North of Tenerife. So, living here gives you lots of options!

Having mentioned the weather, I also have to mention how relaxed it is here. I don't know if it's due to the weather, but everything moves at a slow pace. As an American this is something I had to get used to. I'm from Los Angeles so everything moves rather quickly, but not in Spain unless you live in cities like Madrid or Barcelona, and even then, the speed is still slow by U.S. standards.

Need a Change?

Another reason to move to Spain is that it's a wonderful chance to break up the monotony and try something new. I was tired of the rat race in the U.S. My life consisted of work, study, and work. I barely had any social life and I felt like I had no other purpose but to get up every morning and clock in. I started to research and hear stories about Americans who made a lot of money but left to move to Spain or some other European country. They made a lot less money, but they were happier and they had more free time to do what they wanted. This is something that I craved as I sat at my work desk daydreaming of being anywhere but there.

Speaking of having more time to do what you want; Spain has an incredible work-life balance. Since moving here, I work 30 hours a week and have time to travel to other places on weekends. I should also mention that Spain has a lot of holidays throughout the year. This is because Spain is a Catholic country and most holidays honor Saints. There have been times when I saw people celebrating in the streets and no one was working. I had no clue what they were celebrating and neither did they! Spaniards will find any reason to have fun and enjoy their lives. They say here the people live to work and not work to live. I should also point out that the average job offers 1 month of vacation. 1 month!! I was so shocked when I heard this while I was contemplating my measly two weeks. I even have some friends that get 6 weeks off a year, but this isn't as common as having 4.

Cost of living

The cost of living is another reason why you might want to move here. I was so shocked at how cheap everything was when I first arrived. Of course, everything is cheaper or more expensive depending on which part of Spain you decide to live in. However, the average cost of living is about 34 or 35% less than in the United States. The rent is about 55 or 56% lower. If you live in places like Barcelona, Madrid, or Basque Country then it will be expensive compared to the rest of Spain due to its popularity.

Also, I should mention that if you live in the city center or downtown areas it will be more expensive than living in the outskirts of the city. I was living dead in the center of Madrid and my one-bedroom apartment was about 700 USD a month and that included all the other expenses like water and electricity. When I rented my first apartment in the Canary Islands, I was paying 500 a month and that also included expenses. I have a friend who had a two-bedroom in the Canary Islands that was about 480 a month, but that didn't include the expenses. There are lots of places with cheap rent in mainland Spain as well, especially in Galicia or outside the city centers.

If you like to eat out then you should know that the food and drink are also very cheap. I remember going out with my friends to a shop that sold glasses of wine. It was 1 euro per glass! We got so drunk that night that it was crazy! I should also tell you that in the summertime the food prices will go up due to tourism. This happens a lot in August because that's when everyone wants to come to Spain so the locals will take advantage of the opportunity.

Transportation

One thing that doesn't get mentioned enough is transportation. If you are living in Spain (or anywhere else for that matter) it's going to be important to know your way around. Barcelona and Madrid have some of the best public transportation systems I have ever seen. Both places have an underground metro, a train, and a bus. I've noticed that it's a little cheaper in Barcelona than in Madrid, but both places are cheap. If you want to save money then buy the card that gives you 10 trips instead of buying each trip individually (see figures 1 and 2). In Barcelona, this card is made of paper and in Madrid, it's a plastic red card. You can purchase these tickets at the kiosk inside any metro station

If you don't understand the metro lines you can download apps from the Apple or google play store. In Madrid, I used an app called Metro de Madrid Official. It shows all the lines and colors for each metro. If you want to take the train to Barcelona you will have to buy a separate ticket. The train is called FGC or Ferrocarrils. This train can take you outside the city center. If you prefer to stay in the city center then you don't need this train. However, if you do want to use it then the metro can take you right to the nearest train station. In Madrid, there is another type of metro called Cercanias. You will recognize it due to the backward letter C as its logo. You also need a separate ticket to take these.

If you would like to travel from one city to another, let's say from Madrid to Barcelona then you have two options. You can take the plane or take the train. The train is called the AVE and it's known as a fast-speed train. It's a little on the expensive side. I usually prefer to fly because it's cheaper and faster. However, if you like to see beautiful landscapes as you travel then the AVE might be a better option.

If you plan on living in the Canary Islands, I have some bad news. Although the island life is great, unfortunately, the transportation is not. You have buses on the islands, but they are very slow. If you are a resident of the Canary Islands you can purchase a month pass. You pay 20 euros (20 USD) a month for unlimited trips. I have to recommend getting a car if you want to live in the Canary Islands, because not only is the transportation slow, but some buses don't run as frequently as other buses.

However, if you do live in the Canary Islands as a resident you will receive a 75 percent discount if you take a plane or ferry. This discount applies anywhere you travel in Spain. One day I went to Madrid to visit a friend and my ticket was about 8 euros round trip. For a non-resident, this can be anywhere from 100-300 euros. This is why people who move to the mainland don't want to register their new addresses because if they do, they will lose the discount.

Lastly, I need to mention the price of gasoline. It's a little cheaper in the Canary Islands, but the average price can be between 4-6 dollars a gallon USD. Yeah, the gas is a little on the pricey side especially now with the war between Ukraine and Russia. Speaking of driving, you should know that in Spain there are a lot of narrow roads and roundabouts. I get a little nervous just watching the cars drive down the tiny streets. The streets are very cute for walking and taking Instagram travel pics, but I wouldn't want to drive down them.

These are some of the many reasons why you should consider moving to Spain. Later in the book, I will talk more about these things in further detail. So, when you are finished reading this book you will not only have decided if Spain is right for you, but you'll have a valuable resource and guide that can help you make the transition if that's what you want to do.

Figure 1. Barcelona Travel card with 10 trips

Figure 2. Madrid Travel Card with 10 trips

Chapter 2

Being a Non-EU Citizen

What exactly does being a Non-EU Citizen mean? Some people think it's well…..when you aren't a citizen of a European country. That's technically true, but there is more to it than that. Normally when people refer to EU-Citizens they are talking about people from countries that are part of the European Union. There are about 27 countries in the European Union and Spain is one of them.

So again, what exactly does this mean? Well, it means that these countries have come together politically and economically. They have completely free movement of goods, money, and services. Also, any citizen that is a member of an EU country has the right to move and live freely in any other country of the EU.

I have to stress again that this is a right that only an EU citizen has. If you are from a non-EU country like the U.S. Canada, Mexico, China, etc. then you cannot just pack up and move to Spain without first doing the necessary paperwork and getting a visa. In case you are curious about which countries are part of the European Union here is the list below.

Austria

Belgium

Bulgaria

Croatia

Cyprus

Czech Republic

Denmark

Estonia

Finland

France

Germany

Greece

Hungary

Ireland

Italy

Latvia

Lithuania

Luxembourg

Malta

Netherlands

Poland

Portugal

Romania

Slovakia

Slovenia

Spain

Sweden

If a European country is not on this list, then they are not part of the European Union and they are treated the same as any other country in the world. This also includes the United Kingdom which lost these rights after Brexit.

The Schengen Treaty

People are often confused about the differences between the EU and the Schengen Treaty. The Schengen treaty is an agreement that was signed in the year June of 1985 in a town called Schengen in Luxembourg. This agreement allows its citizens to freely travel to other countries that are also part of the Schengen agreement without any passport checks. The borders are open just like when someone travels from state to state in the U.S. This also means that any non-EU-Citizen can travel from one country to another without going through international passport control checks as long as they are coming from another country that is part of the Schengen agreement. The area of traveling freely without borders is called the Schengen

Zone. So if you were in Spain and decided to travel to Italy you would not have to go through any international border controls. Usually, undocumented people will travel through this area, but would not leave the Schengen Zone because they don't want to get caught without papers.

Non-Schengen Countries

Not every country in the EU is part of the Schengen treaty. This means that even though they are part of the European Union you will still have to go through international border controls. Having said all that, I also have to mention that some countries are part of the Schengen treaty, but not a part of the EU. First, let's list all the Schengen countries so that you know exactly where to travel without dealing with border security. Here is the list below.

Austria

Belgium

The Czech Republic

Denmark

Estonia

Finland

France

Germany

Greece

Hungary

Iceland

Italy

Latvia

Liechtenstein

Lithuania

Luxembourg

Malta

The Netherlands

Monaco (de facto)

Norway

Poland

Portugal

San Marino (de facto)

Slovakia

Slovenia

Sweden

Switzerland

Vatican City (de facto)

Four countries are part of the Schengen treaty, but not part of the EU. Those four countries are listed below.

Iceland

Norway

Switzerland

Liechtenstein

Any country not listed above is not a member of the Schengen agreement and therefore would not have an open border. Keep this in mind should you want to travel around Europe. Having the ability to move without borders makes traveling a lot less stressful.

Chapter 3

Spanish Culture

When you think of Spain what comes to mind? paella? tapas? or sangria? or maybe you think about bullfighting? Well, I hate to break it to you, but Spain is much more than what you see on television. Most of those things are only popular among tourists (except paella) but if you want to fit in like a local you'll have to do away with what you've learned on TV.

Spain is rich in culture and history. Not only did I learn about Spanish culture from friends, but I also had to study it for my Spanish Nationality exam (more on that later). As I mentioned before, Spaniards are very social people. The culture is very close and if you decide to live in Spain, get used to people sitting close to you, talking a lot, and wanting to get to know you. As Americans we tend to like our personal space, well in Spain there is no such thing so be prepared!

Greetings

The very first thing that surprised me when I came to Spain was how the people greeted each other. When people meet it's very common to hug the other person and give two kisses one on each cheek. When a woman tried to do this to me, I originally thought she was being a little too frisky until it was pointed out that this is how Spaniards say hello. I had to admit that at first, it was a little uncomfortable since I'm used to just shaking hands and calling it a day.

Now that I have been living in Spain for so many years, Spanish greetings are completely normal to me. Now my problem is when I travel to the U.S. for vacation thinking I have to greet my fellow Americans with a hug and two kisses like a Spaniard can be very awkward (the last thing I need is a sexual harassment charge).

If you don't feel comfortable at first most people will understand because they know that you are a foreigner, but if you have been living here for a very long time they might not be as forgiving.

The Social Life

I can tell you firsthand that the social life in Spain is not like the United States. The people here are very active. Having said this I should note that there are social and cultural differences between regions which are also called autonomous communities (more on that later). Right now, I'm just speaking in a general sense to give you an idea of what to expect.

When I came to Spain the first thing, I noticed was that people tend to eat outside of restaurants and cafes for a while and just socialize (and gossip). You practically see this everywhere and they will stay there for hours on end talking. There is also a tradition called "sobremesa" that begins usually after a big meal. During Sobremesa friends or family will just sit back at the table, relax and talk. If you go to grocery stores you will find the cashier talking a lot to customers and as an introvert, this was difficult, because I just wanted to purchase my items and leave.

However, now I'm very used to socializing like a Spaniard and often find it fun on days when I have nothing else to do. It's common for a friend to call me and ask to have lunch or a beer and we just sit and have a chat. Due to the social norms in many places, it's very easy to make friends or go out on dates and get to know people. If you don't like to socialize then the best place to live is probably in the Basque Country because they are more introverted than other parts of Spain.

Another thing to mention is that family is very important in Spain. You see families together eating (they don't do TV Trays in the living room) and talking. Having dinner together is important (especially in the south of Spain) and it's common to see fathers and mothers taking turns pushing strollers and carrying babies. Family is number one for most people here and if you make good friends, they too will become your family. I have to admit that watching Spanish families come together is very touching. They even get together to celebrate small things that we usually don't think about.

Spanish Cuisine

One of the best things about Spain is the food. I love Spanish food! Before I get into the cuisine, I have to tell you what Spanish food is not! Spanish food is not Mexican or any other type of Latin American dish! Spanish cuisine is not spicy and is based on a Mediterranean diet. Most food consists of seafood, potatoes, pork, and vegetables. I cannot tell you how many times people told me that they thought Spanish food was the same as Mexican food. Spanish food has more similarities to Portuguese and Italian food than it does to Mexican food. Although some dishes share similar names like tortillas. In Spain a tortilla isn't a round flat piece of bread, it's an egg omelet that's traditionally made with potatoes. A

Spanish omelet is called tortilla españolas, tortilla de patatas or torilla de papas (see figure 3).

Another dish that you might have seen is the famous Paella (see Figure 4). This dish is prepared in a large round pan called a Paellera. Paellera is originally from the region of Valencia located in the southeast of Spain. There are many varieties of this fantastic dish, but it consists of rice with something added to the top like chicken, seafood, snails, vegetables, or even rabbit. Although it's from Valencia, you can find it pretty much everywhere.

Iberian Ham

If you enjoy pork then you will fit right at home in Spain. Ham is very famous throughout Spain, but not just any pork! In Spain and Portugal, there is a breed of pig called the Iberian pig. They are located in the Iberian Peninsula and they are used to make all kinds of dishes. The famous Iberian ham (Jamon Iberico in Spanish) is a place of thinly sliced ham usually taken with red wine and cheese (see Figure 5). The ham usually comes from the leg which can be found in grocery stores hanging on the walls. The ham

is usually cut using a device called a jamonero.

Figure 3. A Potato Spanish Omelet

Figure 4. Seafood Paella

Figure 5. Iberian Ham

Regional Differences

To mention every Spanish dish is beyond the scope of this book, but I would like to mention that what I've said so far has to do with dishes found throughout all parts of Spain. However, each region (like Valencia) has its regional dishes that most foreigners have probably never heard of. To try some of these regional dishes you may have to travel to that specific region. Some regional dishes can be found everywhere like paella or gazpacho (a cold vegetable soup from southern Spain). Speaking of regional dishes, I have to note my favorite Spanish dessert. It's called Paparajotes and it's from a place called Murcia which is in the southeast of Spain. It consists of lemon leaves coated with dough then fired and sprinkled with cinnamon (see Figure 6). If you are ever in Murcia you have to give this dessert a try!

Figure 6. Paparajotes

Chapter 4

Languages of Spain

I'm sure that when you think of Spain you probably think that everyone just speaks Spanish right? Well, this is true to some extent, but did you know that Spanish isn't the only language native to the country? There are several languages spoken in Spain and some of these languages have various dialects, but how is that possible?

Well, many years ago Spain had several kingdoms and each kingdom had its language. The kingdoms slowly started to become one through marriage and other forms of conquest until the kingdom of Castille was left. The language spoken by the kingdom of Castile was called Castilian and this is the Spanish language we know of today. Many people still refer to Spanish as Castilian especially when speaking to elderly people. Spanish or Castilian became the dominant language of the country. The other languages are still spoken today, but they almost went extinct when Spain's former dictator Francisco Franco banned the use of other Spanish languages. However, after he died each region gained the right to speak their language openly so many of the languages survived. Here are a few popular languages still spoken in Spain.

1. Catalan (Spoken in Catalonia, Valencian, and Mallorca with various dialects like Valencian and Mallorquin).

2. Galician (spoken in Galicia located in the northwest of Spain. It was once the same language as Portuguese until it became its separate language.

3. Basque (spoken in the Basque country and is a language Isolate. No one knows exactly where this language originated as it is not a Latin language.

4. Aranese (spoken in the northeast region of Spain and comes from the Occitan language).

5. Silbo (a language used to communicate by whistling. This language is from the original inhabitants of the Canary Islands and is still used today on the Island of La Gomera.

Should You Learn These Languages?

Believe it or not but there are some Spaniards that live in remote areas that don't speak Spanish very well. They speak their regional languages and may struggle to speak Spanish. This is usually the case with elderly people because they have spent most of their lives living in remote rural areas where people didn't speak Spanish.

However, if you are wondering if you should learn these other languages, I would have to say that it depends. It won't be necessary to learn other regional languages unless you love learning languages and would like to take on new challenges. However, there are exceptions to the rule! If you live in places like Catalonia for example, you might want to learn some Catalan. This might also depend on your job because most jobs may require you to speak it. In Valencia, fewer people speak Valencian, but some jobs would also require you to speak the language, but less so than in Catalonia.

I also have to tell you that there are tons of foreigners living in Spain who have never learned Spanish or any other language. I honestly don't understand how people like this can survive because I have always needed to use Spanish in my day-to-day activities. I recommend that you first learn to speak Spanish as it is the number one language spoken in Spain and then you can move on to learning regional languages, but in reality, all you need is Spanish. I know that as Americans we tend to think that everyone speaks English because English is the universal language, but in Spain, this is not the case. If you don't live in a big tourist area then I wish you the best of luck finding anyone that can speak English. So do yourself a favor and at least spend time learning the basics. It will save you a lot of frustration in the long run (speaking from personal experience).

Chapter 5

Learning Spanish

When I came to Spain my Spanish was limited……..very limited. I was only able to say my numbers and a few phrases. I wish that I was better prepared to learn Spanish before I arrived, but sadly that wasn't the case. To make matters worse I was living in remote places where no one spoke a word of English.

However, now I'm fluent in Spanish and I have to admit that it wasn't easy, but it was fun and life-changing. I say life-changing because I was able to make friends by learning Spanish even though my friends didn't speak any English. I will share with you how I learned Spanish and maybe these tips can help you. You should also know that I am very lazy with language learning and don't know how I passed Spanish class in high school.

The first thing I did was buy a language learning program called Rocket Spanish. This program is much better and cheaper than Rosetta Stone. Unfortunately, it teaches Latin American Spanish, but you will learn a lot that can help you survive in Spain. Any Latin American vocabulary I used in Spain was corrected by the people I interacted with. So, to put it simply, it wasn't a problem at all.

Next, I used the most famous app of them all which was Duolingo. This app didn't help me speak, but it did increase my vocabulary and helped me understand grammar. I completed the entire tree of Duolingo in two weeks. I also used google translate and deepl when I was trying to speak to people and couldn't remember certain words.

The next step is the most important of all....SPEAK! yes, that's right you can't be lazy. Spanish has to become a part of your life and it must be used DAILY. I was lucky enough to live with a woman (who is now like a mother to me) who speaks five languages, but not English. She helped me a ton and was kind enough to correct me if I made a mistake. Speaking of corrections, you have to understand that making a mistake is part of the learning process, so don't get discouraged. I've made some pretty embarrassing mistakes that got a few giggles, but people were kind enough to help me.

Ditch English Speaking Friends

One thing I learned was that if you want to learn Spanish you have to make Spanish-speaking friends and avoid people who speak only English. I purposely avoided other Americans and it was difficult at times. It's so easy to walk down the street and hear a familiar accent and then strike up an English conversation. The problem is that you will get too comfortable and then all you'll be speaking is English. You have to leave your comfort zone and make Spanish friends. You will be surprised how many people will try to talk to you even if you don't speak the language yet.

Language Exchanges

A great way to meet people is to go to a language exchange. Language exchanges are usually held in bars. You go meet people and practice languages. I was very nervous at first and it took me a week to have the cojones to go into the bar and strike up a conversation with the locals. You usually spend time speaking English, Spanish, or some other language you want to learn. You can take turns or speak each other's languages the entire time. Some bars also have language games where you can win free alcohol! When I first joined, they offered me a job teaching conversational classes. They paid me and gave me a free beer after each class!

I also made most of my friends this way. I am still very close to my friends and they are amazed at how quickly I learned Spanish. Now when I talk to them Spanish it's all we ever speak. You can find language exchanges all over Spain if you search online or through meetup.com

Watch Cartoons

This may sound silly, but watching cartoons helped me with my listening skills. The cartoon characters speak very basic English which helped train my ear to the words and accents. If you need to use subtitles, what you can do is put on English subtitles first. Once you get better at listening, switch the subtitles to Spanish, and then later when you are more advanced remove the subtitles entirely.

It will also help you to watch cartoons in a category that you find interesting. I enjoy Marvel and DC so I found cartoons in this area that helped a lot and kept me entertained. I was watching movies in Spanish after about three months or so. If you have Netflix even better because they have European Spanish. You might also want to write down any words you don't understand and look up their meaning later.

Books

If you like to read this is a great way to increase vocabulary. The first book I read was the language hacking Spanish Guide by Benny Lewis. This book taught European Spanish so it helped me a lot. There are also some e-books I bought from Amazon Kindle. My favorite author is Ferando Trujillo. His books mostly consist of science fiction, suspense, fantasy, and mystery. If you want to read, please pick a category that you find interesting to prevent boredom.

Use Sticky Notes

Another way to help with vocabulary is to write one word per sticky note and place the note on an object in the house so you can see it each day. So, the table in your dining room should have a note that says mesa. So, every day when you see it you can say the word in your mind. This will help you start to think in Spanish. Speaking of thinking in Spanish, when you engage in self-talk throughout the day, try to use Spanish instead of English. For example, when you think something like "Ugh I have to wake up very early tomorrow" force yourself to mentally say "Ugh tengo que levantarme muy temprano mañana". If you do this every day soon it will become a habit and once it becomes automatic, you will start thinking in Spanish.

The last tip I can give is that when you start to study Spanish try to learn things that you will use in your daily life. You want your vocabulary to reflect what you do daily. Don't start by learning things that you won't use or you'll start to forget pretty quickly. Start learning things that are personal to you so when you introduce yourself to other people you can start by sharing your own story since it will be the easiest to learn. If you like to eat out, learn the basics of ordering your favorite food and use it every time you go to the restaurant. If you follow these tips, you will be speaking fluently in no time.

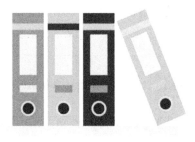

Chapter 6

Spanish Bureaucracy

As Americans, we like to do things in a hurry. We want to go in and out of a place quickly so that we can run other errands. Well, I have to warn you right now that this is not the case in Spain. One problem I had when I first arrived was how bad the Spanish bureaucracy was. I remember reading on the internet that many people (including other Spaniards) were complaining about how Spain handles things.

Spain does everything slowly and usually there is a lot of paperwork involved. I remember how I hated going to the bank because every single time I needed something I would be there for hours on end. Sometimes I would have to wake up early just to run my errands and avoid long lines and slow waiting times. It doesn't matter what you have to do in Spain, just expect to wait a while for everything. This also includes calling a business and being put on hold. I should note that if you call a business and leave a message, they might not even call you back.

Unorganized

Spain also lacks the same organization that we have in the States. I remember when I tried to open a bank account online and the bank asked me to fill out a few papers and email them to them. I waited for a month and then they told me I was missing documents. They gave me the document, and then after another month, they told me I was missing another document. After three and half months they finally opened my bank account. However, I didn't receive my debit card until another two months because they forgot to mail it like they said they would. So, I had to wait five and a half months before I could use my account.

I have been frustrated with everything I had to do in Spain, from opening a bank account to buying groceries. When I had to get my documentation for my residency, I had to collect a lot of paperwork, and when I went to the police to get my ID card, they asked a bunch of questions to see if I had everything. Luckily for me, I spent most of my time double-checking everything before I went there. If you have to do anything that requires paperwork, make sure you do your research and have more documents than what they ask because they will most likely tell you that you are missing something. If they say you need five passport copies, make ten instead. If you overdo it with the paperwork, you won't have any room for error.

Laziness

There are stereotypes about Spaniards being lazy. There is some truth to this when it comes to Spanish bureaucracy. I've seen more laziness in the Canary Islands than anywhere else in Spain. It feels as if no one wants to work, and they will take their time as if they are on vacation. You can wait in line, and the workers will stop and constantly talk to their co-workers about how drunk Jose Antonio was at the party last night or some other type of gossip that could be talked about during lunch. My Spanish friends also get upset about this and they are used to it. As an American, this still irritates me even to this very day.

When you come to Spain, you have to register your address with the city hall, and they will give you a certificate called an empadronamiento. One day I had to get another certificate because I couldn't find my old one. The lady asked to see my ID and asked me three times if I was American (although it says U.S. on the ID card). I told her yes three times, and then she told me to wait while she printed another certificate. I waited forty-five minutes for her to print out a piece of paper! She kept talking to her co-worker about the local gossip, and I was just sitting there mentally swearing at her in my head.

Patience

The biggest takeaway here is to have patience because you'll need it. Understand that you are in a different country with different rules. Always be prepared, double-check everything, and always have more than what's requested. Understand that you will also be waiting for a while so it's best to get an early start and plan your day accordingly.

Chapter 7

Autonomous Communities

Before you decide to pack up and leave you may want to investigate Spain's autonomous communities. There are 17 autonomous communities in Spain and each community has its own set of laws, governments, languages, dialects, gastronomy, and cultures. You can think of them as different states in the U.S. I know when we think of other countries, we don't consider the regional differences, but each region is almost like a different country within a county. In this book, I try to give a general view of Spain, but remember that apart from this you will still have to know the laws of the region you decide to live in, this is especially true when you have to pay taxes. The names of each community are

Andalusia

Aragón

Balearic Islands

Basque Country

Canary Islands

Cantabria

Castilla and Leon

Castilla-La Mancha

Catalonia

Community of Madrid

Extremadura

Galicia

La Rioja

Navarre

Principality of Asturias

Region of Murcia

Valencian Community

Apart from these, there are two autonomous cities called Ceuta and

Melilla.

Andalusia

The biggest region in Spain by far is Andalusia. It's the

home to flamenco and gazpacho! The capital of Andalusia is Seville.

There are eight provinces located in Andalusia. Cádiz, Córdoba,

Granada, Huelva, Jaén, Málaga and Seville. If you like warmer climates then Andalusia is probably the best place to be in the peninsula. However, in the summer it can be very hot, especially in Seville. The people are very social and energetic so if you are an extrovert this is probably the place for you.

Aragón

In the northeast of Spain, you will find Aragon. Zaragoza is the capital and although the people speak Spanish you will find people who speak Catalan and Aragonese in the Pyrenees Valley region. Aragonese is a Latin-based language with several dialects spoken throughout the area.

Balearic Islands

If you enjoy the Island life then the Balearic Islands might be a good option. There are five islands to choose from which are Cabrera, Formentera, Ibiza, Mallorca and Menorca. The official languages are Spanish and Mallorquin which is a dialect of Catalan. I'm sure you may have heard that Ibiza is the party Island. This is true as many foreigners go to Ibiza to party and have a good time, but this is also why it's one of the most expensive islands to live or visit.

Basque Country

Basque Country is very unique. It's located in the north and shares a border with France. In addition to speaking Spanish, they speak a language called Basque which is not related to any Latin language. It's considered to be a language isolate with unknown origins. This region is also very green with colder temperatures and more rain like other regions in the north. There are also three provinces located in Basque Country, Alava, Guipúzcoa, and

Biscay. How you pronounce these places is anybody's guess.

Canary Islands

I have been living in the Canary Islands for more than four

years now and I can tell you that it's a very beautiful and quiet

place. There are seven Islands (some say eight) located to the west

of Morocco. The Islands are

Fuerteventura

Gran Canaria

Lanzarote

La Gomera

La Palma

El Hierro

Tenerife

The islands have a subtropical climate so it's warm pretty much all year around. The people here have accents that are very similar to Latin Americans, especially Venezuelans. If you want the best weather in Spain with a Caribbean vibe then come to the Canary Islands. I can promise you won't be disappointed.

Cantabria

Cantabria is also located in the northern region of Spain with Santander as its capital. Cantabria is very green with cold temperatures. It's a very beautiful place to visit for vacation and to live if you don't mind the rain. It's located west of Basque Country. There used to be a language called montañes which is a dialect of another language called Astur-Leonese. The language is considered to be endangered.

Castilla and Leon

One of my favorite places in Spain is Castilla and Leon. Valladolid is its capital and it is known to be the biggest region of

Spain. It used to be a separate kingdom many centuries ago. The nine provinces are

Avila

Burgos

Leon

Palencia

Segovia

Soria

Salamanca

Valladolid

If you like to see big ancient castles then you will love Castilla and Leon. The weather is a bit cold at times, but it's an amazing place. Also, if you are just learning Spanish, Castilla, and Leon has the most clear, understandable, and neutral Spanish in the entire country.

Castilla-La Mancha

With Toledo as its capital, Castilla-La Mancha is known to have great vineyards, castles, and windmills. It's next to Madrid and Valencia and famous provinces include

Albacete

Ciudad Real

Cuenca

Guadalajara

They also say that it's a very good area to teach English because of the high demand. Also, I have to add that the public transportation system is excellent! You won't need a car to move around this region.

Catalonia

Also located in the northeast of the peninsula you will find the autonomous region of Catalonia. The people in this region speak Spanish and Catalan. There are four cities which are Barcelona the capital followed by Girona, Lleida, and Tarragona. Barcelona is one of the most well-known places in Spain, but the other cities are just as beautiful and worth exploring. The government of Catalonia was dissolved after they tried to vote for independence from Spain. According to the Spanish government, this was an illegal act and a

66

few Catalonia officials were sent to prison causing the government to collapse.

Community of Madrid

Madrid is situated directly in the center of Spain and is considered the country's capital. The transportation system (along with Barcelona) is the best I have ever seen in my life. The city is very metropolitan and there are many things to do. The nightlife is also very active. The weather is a bit dry and extreme. In the winter it's very cold and in the summer it's very hot. Sometimes it can snow in the winter. Snow isn't very common, but it has happened. If you are a city person then you will feel at home living in Madrid.

Keep in mind that Madrid and Barcelona are some of the most expensive cities in Spain.

Extremadura

You can find Extremadura to the west of Spain next to Portugal. It has two of the largest provinces in Spain which are Badajoz and Caceres. Other cities include its capital Merida and Plasencia. The great part about living here is that you can always drive to Portugal on the weekends and come back to Spain just before work!

Galicia

If you like seafood then head on over to Galicia because it's known for having the best seafood in the entire country. This beautiful green region is located in the Pacific Northwest of Spain and north of Portugal. The languages spoken are Spanish and Galician, which is a language very similar to Portuguese (actually Galician and Portuguese used to be the same language).

Galicia has four provinces with its capital city being Santiago de Compostela. A Coruña, Lugo Ourense, and Pontevedra are the four provinces worth visiting but be warned that the weather is a bit gray and rainy with cold water beaches.

La Rioja

Located in the Northeast of Spain with Logroño as its capital. La Rioja is very beautiful. My favorite red wine in Spain is called La Rioja and it is delicious. I recommend you give it a try if you enjoy red wine. La Rioja is known for producing a lot of wine and here you can find many vineyards. La Rioja shares its northern border with Basque Country.

Navarre

Navarre is located in the north of Spain and south of France. The capital is called Pamplona and, in some parts, you can find people speaking Basque (usually in the north). There is only one province which is called Navarre.

Principality of Asturias

You can find Asturias in the northern part of Spain. Oviedo is its capital and it's close to the sea of Cantabria. There are a few regional dishes to try like faba asturiana and cachopo. There are also a few cities to visit like Avilés, Gijón, Langreo, Llanes, and Mieres.

Region of Murcia

If you prefer the Mediterranean Sea then Murcia might be what you are looking for as it's right off the coast of the Mediterranean in the southeast of Spain. Murcia is the seventh largest region in Spain with a population of more than 1,334,431 inhabitants. The weather is generally hot with mild winters.

Valencian Community

Home to the most well-known dish called Paella, Valencia is located in the east of Spain. Its capital is also called Valencia and the official languages are Spanish and Valencian (a debated dialect of Catalan). To my surprise, there aren't a lot of people that speak Valencian as there are Catalan speakers in Catalonia. Valencia is one of the regions with a strong economy and higher employment rates. The transportation system is also very good. You can take the Ferrocarrils de la Generalitat Valenciana

(FGV) or the Estació de Valencia-Joaquin Sorolla, which is very similar to the AVE train.

Chapter 8

Security and Safety

The last time I read the global peace index of 2022 (which was a week ago) I saw that Spain was given a rank of 29 which is better than what it was last year. To give you an idea of how well 29 rank stands, the United States was given a rank of 129. So, it's safe to say that Spain is a much more peaceful place than the U. S.

When we travel to other countries, we have many questions about safety and security. Living in Spain gave me a sense of freedom that I didn't have in the U.S. In Spain, I could walk the streets of Madrid at four in the morning without any fear of being shot or robbed. You never hear about mass shootings or gun violence in Spain because guns are well…..banned. When I first arrived in Barcelona, I was told to be careful because there is a lot of pick pocketers there. This is a sad truth, but this is one of the biggest crimes in the city.

I was relieved because I can deal with pick pocketers, but someone with a gun is another story. I did have someone try to pickpocket me on the metro once. They thought they were sneaky when trying to open my backpack as if I couldn't feel the movements. They quickly stopped when I turned around and gave them a dirty look and that was about it.

Drugs

I do have to say that I have seen an issue with drugs, especially cocaine. There have been a lot of drug trafficking cases on the news and in the Canary Islands there was a plane stopped in the Island of Fuerteventura that was filled with cocaine that came from South America. I have also seen the civil guard stop boats off the cost of the Canaries that were transporting cocaine from North Africa.

I'm not sure if Spain has the resources to fix this issue, but it is a known issue in the country. People find creative ways to move drugs in and out of the country. There were recently two women who were stopped going through airport security in Colombia because they were hiding vials of cocaine in their hair extensions. They were headed to Madrid.

Violence

Although violence is rare in Spain it's not unheard of. I have seen the occasional drunken fights at nightclubs, women upset that their boyfriends were talking to other women, or two men fighting over the same girl. In Spain, the first person that draws blood is usually the one that goes to jail.

There have also been a few murders that shocked the entire country. A boy was beaten to death in Madrid for being gay. The entire country was in shock as Spain has been for the most part a very gay-friendly country. I should add that the people who killed the boy were foreigners. I can tell you that this is not a common occurrence because Spain is very used to openly gay people and was one of the first countries in the world to approve gay marriage.

A few years ago in Fuerteventura, there was a body of a woman found with her breast removed. The police believe that it was a drug deal gone wrong. The woman was from Latin America and they never caught her killer. They believe that the person responsible had been long gone and out of the country.

Be Vigilant

Having said all this I do want to say that these incidents are very uncommon, but you do want to pay attention to the news and be aware of any new changes. Watch the local news and read the local newspapers (which you can find online). If you don't speak Spanish (and I hope you try to learn) you can find many resources online in English. If you come from the United States you might

have to get used to the level of safety, security, and peace that Spain

provides, but I can promise you that you will love it and worry less!

Chapter 9

Finding Work

Unless you are retired or rich, you will probably look for work once you arrive in Spain. I have to be honest and say that if you are a non-EU citizen it will be more difficult to find work. The reason for this is that EU citizens get priority when it comes to jobs since they are members of the EU. For a Spanish company to hire you they would have to explain why they chose you over an EU member and this can be difficult even for them. Their decision would also involve a lot more paperwork, which for this reason alone would be simply reason enough to just hire someone from the EU.

Although finding work is a bit more difficult as a non-EU citizen it's not impossible. If you are already a legal resident then it won't be an issue at all since they wouldn't need less paperwork and you would also be on the same level as an EU citizen. What I mean by difficult is that if you are trying to come to Spain on a work visa. If you have a really important job like a scientist or doctor then you probably wouldn't have any issues getting sponsored, but if you are in retail or something then you can probably forget about it.

Teaching English

Have you ever noticed when you see foreigners move to other countries, they tend to gravitate towards certain jobs like taxi driver or cleaner? Well, Americans are no exception. We tend to gravitate towards teaching English. This is usually because it's one of the easiest jobs to do in Spain. You don't even have to speak

Spanish although some schools may want you to have a basic level, but generally, it's not required.

Becoming an English teacher is quite simple. You need a bachelor's degree and a teaching certificate. The certificate can be anything from a TEFL, TESOL, CELTA, etc. It should have at least 120 hours or more along with practicum experience. You can get these certificates online or in the classrooms. Some schools offer student visas which will also allow you to work legally. Another reason why people teach English is because there is a high demand for English teachers in Spain. There are lots of Language Assistant programs that can place you in a school and provide you with a visa (this is probably the easiest way to live legally in Spain). There is also a downside to teaching English that I should mention. The pay is relatively low depending on where you are and who you are teaching. Most people are looking for teachers to teach children, but the highest earners teach Business English. You can also create your salary by teaching private lessons instead of teaching in a classroom or you can teach online. The possibilities are endless. However, if you are looking to get a teaching certificate make sure the school is accredited. Look for things like TQUK, ACCET, or College of Teachers. If you go through a university that is accredited then the certificate will also have the proper accreditation. Below is a list of accredited schools.

International TEFL Academy

i-to-i TEFL

The Language House TEFL

Premier TEFL

Oxford TEFL

myTEFL

International TEFL and TESOL Training

Job Searching Sites

If you don't yet speak Spanish there are other jobs that you can do. These jobs mostly fall in the tourism sector like hotels, restaurants, etc. However, if you don't have legal residency then it will be very difficult to get sponsored. There are a few sites to search for jobs and some might sponsor you if you don't have papers so you might want to give them a try. Below is a list of a few sites to find work.

Lingo Bongo (for teaching English in Madrid and Barcelona)

Good Air Language (for online teaching jobs)

OET Jobs (for online teaching jobs)

Trabajos.com (for Spanish non-teaching jobs)

InfoJobs (for non-teaching jobs)

Linkedin (for all jobs)

Chapter10

Spanish Healthcare

I'm sure if you're considering moving to Spain you might be wondering about the healthcare system. This is a valid concern and I have to say that in my experience the Spanish healthcare system is quite good. It's not perfect, but you will learn that you have a lot of options. Unlike the U. S. Spanish citizens and residents have both private healthcare insurance and universal healthcare.

Universal Healthcare

Spain has what is known as the National Health System. This means that all citizens and legal foreign residents are entitled to healthcare services regardless if they are employed or not. The primary healthcare center is generally where you would go to get treated. These centers are called the Centro de Salud. Depending on your income you may have to pay co-pays or some other type of fee, but because the healthcare system is subsidized it is extremely affordable to everyone. If you need a prescription the cost would also vary depending on your income level. I also want to note that Universal Healthcare is the same in all autonomous communities of Spain regardless of where you decide to live.

Private Healthcare

Spain also offers private healthcare which is similar to what is available in the United States. Private healthcare gives you access to private hospitals that accept private healthcare insurance. There are many ways to get private access to private healthcare insurance. You can contact the provider directly, be added to your significant others' plan if they have it, or even through a bank. When I first arrived in Spain, I was offered private healthcare through my bank when I opened an account. The bank I used was BBVA and they offered healthcare through a company called Sanitas and I was paying about 500 euros a year. Keep in mind that the price goes up with age.

Many private healthcare companies offer various plans with coverage ranging from health, dental, and vision. You don't even have to be a resident to get private healthcare. Many companies will provide you with healthcare using just a passport. Here is a list of a few private healthcare providers in Spain.

Adeslas

Asisa

Cigna

Mapfre

Sanitas

I have personally only used Sanitas and Adeslas and have found both to be very good. You may have to consult different providers to see which is best for you. I rarely go to the doctor, but it's nice to know that I have so many options available. If you apply for a visa, you most likely will need private healthcare insurance. So, I hope this list helps, but there are a lot more providers than what I have listed here. I also want to add that you cannot use private healthcare insurance at the Centro de Salud. You will have to find a private healthcare facility in your area.

Chapter 11

Getting a Visa

If you are an American or a non-EU citizen, you must obtain a visa if you plan on living in Spain. Of course, if you are American and you want to visit Spain as a tourist then you don't need a visa, but this lasts only up to 90 days. After 90 days you either have to get a visa or leave the EU. I'll have to be honest with you and say that getting a visa is not easy for many people, but it's not impossible. Let's look at some of our available options.

Visas for Digital Nomads

If you work remotely then you are more than halfway to getting a visa. I would have to say that the digital nomad visa is probably the easiest to get due to the minimum requirements needed. This visa was specifically made for non-EU-Citizens and it will allow you to stay in Spain for one year if you apply outside of Spain. If you apply within Spain, you can get a visa for three years. If you do have a one-year permit you can always modify it to three years once you arrive in Spain. This visa also counts towards Spanish citizenship.

You can renew this visa and once you have resided in Spain legally for 5 years then you can obtain a permanent resident card which will allow you to stay in Spain indefinitely. Also, this visa will allow you to travel to other EU countries without any restrictions. Now you may be asking what are the requirements? well let's take a look, shall we?

Requirements for the Digital Nomad Visa

If you are interested in the visa for digital nomads first you have to be one of two types of people. The first is if you work for a company remotely and the other is if you are self-employed with clients from different parts of the world receiving income from different places (except Spain).

You must show that at least 80% of your income is from companies outside of Spain or from a non-Spanish company. The remaining 20% can be from Spain or a Spanish company. You will need to show that you have been with the company for at least one year before submitting your application. If you are self-employed you will have to show that you have had your clients for more than 3 months.

All documentation must be legalized and apostilled. This includes your criminal records which you cannot have or you won't be able to get the visa. You also cannot be barred from entering Spain or the European Union in general. When you submit your criminal record, it has to be valid for at least 90 days. Also, your criminal history has to go back for at least 5 years.

If you have lived in Spain before then you know that you will also need private health insurance with full coverage. Several healthcare companies can help you. I used to have Sanitas, but now I have Adeslas

Education

To apply for the visa, you must either have a graduate or postgraduate degree from an accredited university (doesn't matter what subject) or vocational training. If you don't meet the educational requirements the other option is to show that you have 3 years work-related experience in your remote job before you apply.

Bank Certificate

You will be obligated to show that you have at least 25k euros and 9,441 euros for each additional person that is coming with you. You can do this by showing your job contract or the money from your bank account, but the statements will have to be translated. There is also an administrative fee to be paid.

Final Requirements

If you are working for a company then the company has to have been operational for at least a year. The contract must also state that you are allowed to work remotely. If you are a freelancer you have to work for one company minimum with the contract specifically stating that you are a remote worker.

Student Visa

The next visa that might interest you is a student visa. This visa allows you to live legally in Spain for either a short-term or long-term period. You can study at a university, work as an intern, train, or participate in a student exchange. If you're American and would like to stay in Spain for less than three months then you can still study during that time without a student visa. However, if you want to stay longer, then you will have to get a visa. A short-term visa allows you to stay in Spain for up to 6 months and anything longer than that will require a long-term visa. I also have to add that a student visa will allow you to work up to 20 hours per week.

Required Documents

The requirements to get a student visa are pretty straightforward. First, you have to be accepted to a school and prove it by showing an acceptance letter. The studies can be in any subject or any educational institution. At the end of each academic year, you will have to renew the visa. Although you are allowed to work on the visa you will still have to show that you will be able to financially support yourself during the academic year and your main source of income cannot be from the job you landed while using the student visa.

The job won't count towards the funds needed to show that you can support yourself while in Spain. Also, you must know that your work cannot interfere with your study hours.

Here is a list of the documents you will need when applying for a student visa,

Health Insurance

Proof funds to cover your stay such as bank statements etc.

Current Student ID

ID Card (passport driver's license etc).

Acceptance Letter

A Valid **Passport** (that won't expire while you are in Spain).

2 Schengen Visa Application Forms

Non-Lucrative Visa

Another easy visa option is the non-lucrative visa. This type of visa will allow you to stay legally in Spain for up to one year. After one year has passed you can renew it for up to two years and of course, after five years you can switch to become a permanent resident. This visa will allow you to bring your married or unmarried partner along with any children or dependents that you may have.

Although the visa is easy to obtain, the downside is that you cannot work using this visa. You have to show that you have sufficient means of taking care of yourself and your dependents while using this visa. At this moment you will need to have at least 28,800 euros in your bank account. This can change at any time so please keep this in mind. This visa is very attractive for those who are retired and receiving some sort of pension. To prove you have the funds a certificate from your bank may be required or/and bank statements for the last six months of your application. Also, keep in mind that the money doesn't have to come from one bank. If you decide to bring anyone with you to Spain, you will need an additional 6,454.03 euros for each additional family member along with private health insurance (see chapter:10). The health insurance must be from a company in Spain with at least one year of full coverage.

The last thing I want to mention is that if you do decide to get a non-lucrative visa you cannot start the process in Spain. Everything has to be done at the Spanish Consulate in your home country. Once it is approved then you have no more than three months to relocate to Spain and finish the process to get your foreign ID. Once you arrive, you'll have 1 month to get the ID after you register your address with the city hall, so don't waste any time because, as I mentioned before, the bureaucracy in Spain is horrible.

Once all this is done, you should receive your residency card within 40 days.

Chapter 12

Finding Housing

If you plan to move to Spain, you'll likely be looking for a place to live. The process can be daunting whether you're buying or renting. This is because of the bureaucracy that I spoke about earlier. I know so many people who have looked for a place, and the landlord never returned their calls or responded to their e-mails. If you want the landlord or seller's attention, you'll have to call as if they owe you money.

Usually, if you are looking to rent an apartment, some landlords may want up to 3 months' rent upfront. However, this depends on the company and the laws of the autonomous community. Due to high tourism, many landlords are now only offering vocational or short-term rentals. I also have to add that the prices of renting an apartment vary drastically. If you're thinking about living in Barcelona or Madrid, please know that the rent is the most expensive, especially in the downtown areas.

Buying a House

For those who would like to buy a home, please note that if you are not a resident, your taxes will be much higher. If you are a single first-time home buyer, then the bank will pay up to 80% of the house's value. However, if you're buying a house with your partner or a second home, then they will pay up to 60%. Some banks may pay up to 90%, but this is rare. If you aren't a resident, the real estate agents will help you get a Spanish bank account and a tax ID number. The tax ID number will not make you a resident as some people believe.

Here is a list of places you can use to find a place to rent or buy,

Idealista

Fotocasa

Habitaclia

Pisos.com

Kyero

Yaencontre

Globaliza

SpainHouses

ThinkSpain

Mil Anuncios

Trovit

Enalquiler

Vibbo

Green-Acres

Chapter 13

Residency by Marriage

Let's say you fall in love with a Spaniard and like to get married, but you aren't a resident. Well, you can still get married, but there will be a few things you will have to do first. I will give you the general outline, but make sure you double-check the autonomous community where the marriage will take place just to make sure there are no additional requirements.

The first thing you'll need is your birth certificate with the apostille stamp. This has to be done in your home country, not in Spain. Next, you have to have it translated by a professional. I had mine done in Spain and they asked me to send photocopies via email to them. Then they translated it and sent me the translated copies through mail and email. Also, note that the birth certificate can't be older than 3 months.

You will also need copies of your passport. I made a copy of every page just to be safe. Then you will need a paper that says that you're single and free to marry. The United States does not have this so you will have to go to the nearest U.S. embassy or consulate and sign a document saying that you are single and also pay a fee. The document will be in Spanish so you won't need to have it legalized or translated. You will also need to have an empadronamiento that shows you have been living in Spain for the last two years. You get that document when you register your address at the city hall. If you don't have this document then the U.S. Embassy or consulate will give you a form to write down your previous addresses for the last two years. Lastly, you will need a copy of your significant other's DNI card. Take everything to the civil registry and then they will give you the marriage date, congrats!

The Residency Process

Once you tie the knot you will have to take the marriage certificate to the foreigners' office (extranjería). Also, you'll have to bring photos of all passport pages, the empadronamiento, a copy of your partner's DNI, and the family book (if they are still issuing those). After this is done you will receive a temporary residency permit in the mail. You must keep this paper with you at all times until you receive permanent residency. If they approve your residency, you will be notified by mail.

The next step is to download a paper online (all of the instructions will be in the mail notification) and pay a fee of 12 euros. Take this paper to the national police along with 3 passport-size photos. The police will give you two papers and then you have to wait 3 months and then go back to the police station to get your residency card. You will have to show them the papers they gave you to get the card. The card will have your photo and your NIE on it. After that, you will be a legal resident! Oh, and one other important thing is that you cannot leave the country more than 3 months out of the year!

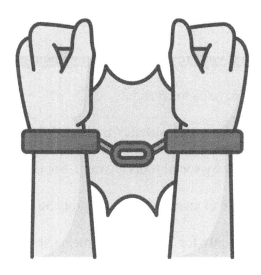

Chapter 14

Living Illegally

Before I begin, I have to state that I am not recommending to anyone that they come to Spain illegally. However, some people do make it to Spain and overstay their visas or come through some other means. Spain calls this an irregular situation and I have seen it with a lot of people outside the EU. Luckily Spain has things in place to help those in this type of situation. So, yes you can become a resident even if you are living in Spain without papers. However, there are many caveats to consider.

Residency by Social Roots

Residency by social roots (Arraigo Social) is probably the easiest route you can take, but the only problem is that you have to live in Spain illegally for 3 years. This means that you cannot leave the country for any reason. If you do decide to leave the country you may not be able to go back. You must keep a record of everything you have done since living in the country to show that you have been living here for 3 years.

The best way to show proof is to keep every empadronamiento you receive from the city hall. Also don't worry about registering your address at the city hall if you are undocumented. They won't report you, but they do need to know how many people are living in that particular area. In addition to this keep other forms of documentation like library cards, receipts, etc. Arraigo social means social roots and you will be required to show

Spain that you have integrated into Spanish society during your 3-year stay.

When you are ready to apply for residency through arraigo social you don't need to go back to your home country. You can do everything in Spain and save a ton of money by not booking a flight. Normally they would expect you to have a work contract for at least a year and if you have family ties to someone in the country this will also help. If you don't have any of those then you will have to show that you have enough financial means to support yourself. I remember when one of my bosses helped an employee who didn't have paperwork. She contacted her lawyer who provided all the instructions, but she decided to return to her country due to family reasons so she never applied for arraigo social.

There are a few more documents you will need to show which would be a clean criminal background check from Spain and your home country. I also want to add that arraigo social is only for non-EU citizens. You also cannot be prohibited from entering Spain or you will be automatically rejected. Lastly, you will have to fill out a form called Modelo official (EX-10) which can be found on Spain's official government website.

Arraigo Laboral

Arraigo Laboral is gaining residency by having a work contract in Spain. This means that you have been living in Spain illegally and working under the table for at least 6 months and you can prove it. The process is similar to arraigo social but with two exceptions. First, the time spent in Spain is reduced to two years instead of three. The second is that you will be required to report your employer to the authorities for hiring you without paperwork.

Most people don't use arraigo laboral because they don't want to report their employer so they work another year and file for arraigo social. Once you report your employer there will be an investigation to make sure that you were working illegally and then they will take the appropriate actions against your employer.

If you do find yourself in an irregular situation it is up to you which route you want to take. Both routes have their pros and cons, but remember to save and record everything that you do while in

Spain. You will need as much proof as possible to show that you have been here without papers. Also, keep in mind that even if you do take these routes the government can still deny your application.

Chapter 15

Gaining Spanish Citizenship

If you have been living in Spain legally for a while you may decide that one day you would like to become a Spanish citizen. There are many reasons why someone would become a citizen. Citizens can vote and they don't have to update a residency card every few years. You also become an EU citizen and can live in other EU countries without doing a lot of paperwork

However, there are many ways to gain Spanish citizenship. Marriage is the obvious choice if you are married to a Spanish citizen. You should have to be married for at least one year before you can apply. If you aren't married you can get citizenship if you're a resident, but the wait time depends on your country of origin.

If you come from a country that was colonized by Spain or from countries like Portugal or Andorra then you would have to be a resident for two years before you can apply. It's also two years if you are Sephardic Jewish. If you have at least one Spanish grandparent then the wait time would be a year. If you have a parent then you don't have to wait at all (this also includes people who were adopted by a Spaniard). However, if you don't have either of the things, I've listed then the wait time will be 10 years before you can apply. I know that's incredibly long, but that's what Spain has decided. On top of the waiting times after you apply you are supposed to wait another year before receiving a response, but due to the bureaucracy, some people have waited for 2 or 3 years before receiving a response. Let's take a look at what you will need before you can even apply.

Depending on which route you take to get nationality you will need either the marriage certificate (if married and your partner's birth certificate) or birth certificates to show ancestry (if it's through a parent or grandparent). If you are not from a country that speaks Spanish then you will have to take an A-2 Spanish test through the Institute of Cervantes called the DELE exam. You will also be required to take the cultural test called the CCSE exam. The CCSE has 25 questions all multiple-choice. You can download the app to your phone which has all the questions that could show up on the exam as well as practice tests.

You will need a legalized and translated copy of a criminal background check from your country of origin and from Spain (you can get the Spanish certificate from the Ministry of Justice office) no older than 6 months from when you apply. You will also need your birth certificate legalized and translated. Lastly, you will need your empadronamiento from the city hall, a copy of your passport pages, a copy of your NIE, and the application fee. If you don't receive a response after one year, you can apply to appeal the process through an immigration lawyer to speed things up.

Conclusion

In conclusion, this comprehensive guide offers a personal and in-depth exploration of what it means to live in Spain as a non-EU citizen. It goes beyond the surface-level attractions of the country, delving into the intricacies and practicalities that can greatly impact one's experience and integration into Spanish society.

Living in a country like Spain, with its rich history, diverse landscapes, and warm Mediterranean climate, can be an incredibly fulfilling and transformative experience. However, it's important to navigate the unique challenges that non-EU citizens may face, and this guide is designed to provide the necessary tools and knowledge to do just that.

From understanding why Spain is such an appealing destination, to unraveling the complexities of being a non-EU citizen, this guide aims to shed light on the realities and opportunities that await you. It delves into the vibrant Spanish culture, helping you embrace the customs, traditions, and way of life that define this remarkable nation.

Language is a powerful tool for connection and integration, and this guide emphasizes the significance of learning Spanish. It offers insights into the different languages spoken within Spain and provides practical advice on how to navigate the journey of language acquisition.

The bureaucratic processes can be overwhelming, but fear not! This guide walks you through the maze of Spanish bureaucracy, ensuring that you are equipped with the knowledge and resources to navigate it successfully. It also highlights the unique characteristics of the autonomous communities, offering a deeper understanding of Spain's regional identities and cultural diversity.

Ensuring your safety and security is of paramount importance, and this guide provides valuable information and tips to help you feel confident and protected while living in Spain. It also offers practical guidance on finding employment, as well as insights into the Spanish healthcare system, ensuring that your well-being is taken care of.

Obtaining a visa and finding suitable housing are vital steps in your journey, and this guide provides valuable advice to make the process smoother. It also explores options such as residency by marriage and sheds light on the challenges and implications of living in Spain illegally.

Finally, the guide explores the path to gaining Spanish citizenship, a significant milestone that opens doors to greater opportunities and a sense of belonging. By providing information and guidance on this topic, it empowers you to take the necessary steps toward full integration into Spanish society.

In essence, this guide aims to be your trusted companion, providing you with a comprehensive understanding of what it takes to live, work, and thrive in Spain as a non-EU citizen. It offers insights, tips, and personal anecdotes to help you make informed decisions and embark on a fulfilling journey in this captivating country. So, seize the opportunity, immerse yourself in the Spanish way of life, and let this guide be your compass as you navigate the

remarkable adventure that awaits you in Spain.

About the Author

Kai Cesaire, a spirited individual, has spent the past six years residing in Spain. His adventurous spirit has led him on countless travels throughout Europe, where he passionately imparts his knowledge of English and shares his experiences of living in Spain.

During his time in Spain, Kai has embraced the vibrant culture and diverse landscapes of the country. From the bustling streets of Madrid to the enchanting coastal towns of Barcelona, he has immersed himself in the rich tapestry of Spanish life. However, Kai's thirst for exploration extends beyond Spain's borders as he ventures throughout Europe, constantly seeking new adventures and encounters.

As an English teacher, Kai utilizes his language skills to connect with people from various backgrounds. His warm and approachable nature allows him to form meaningful connections, bridging the gap between different cultures. With enthusiasm, Kai imparts his knowledge of Spain, sharing stories about traditional fiestas, offering insider tips on the best tapas joints, and providing invaluable insights into Spanish customs.

Kai's firsthand experiences have made him a well-rounded guide, capable of showcasing the multifaceted aspects of Spanish life. Whether he is marveling at the architectural wonders of Barcelona's Sagrada Familia or meandering through the charming streets of Seville's Santa Cruz neighborhood, his passion for Spain shines through as he enthusiastically recounts his own adventures.

Through his dedication to teaching and sharing knowledge, Kai strives to cultivate an appreciation for the Spanish way of life. He encourages others to step outside their comfort zones, embrace new experiences, and develop a deeper understanding of Spanish culture. Kai Cesaire's journey is one of discovery, connection, and a genuine desire to foster cultural exchange. His impact extends far beyond his own life, leaving an indelible mark on those fortunate enough to cross paths with him.

Made in the USA
Las Vegas, NV
15 December 2024

14247987R00069